DIGITAL FREELANCING FOR WOMEN AT HOME

WANT TO EARN MONEY SITTING AT THE COMFORT OF YOUR HOME OR AS A SIDE GIG?

JAYASTY ANANDAN

Copyright © Jayasty Anandan
All Rights Reserved.

This book has been published with all efforts taken to make the material error-free after the consent of the author. However, the author and the publisher do not assume and hereby disclaim any liability to any party for any loss, damage, or disruption caused by errors or omissions, whether such errors or omissions result from negligence, accident, or any other cause.

While every effort has been made to avoid any mistake or omission, this publication is being sold on the condition and understanding that neither the author nor the publishers or printers would be liable in any manner to any person by reason of any mistake or omission in this publication or for any action taken or omitted to be taken or advice rendered or accepted on the basis of this work. For any defect in printing or binding the publishers will be liable only to replace the defective copy by another copy of this work then available.

Contents

Preface

When I see through my eyes, I see several women like YOU facing challenges in every phase of their life. I had a strong intuition that this problem can be solved if YOU get the right direction and act on it.

It's my privilege to write this book and help as many women as possible (to be financially free).

What if I tell you the hack to earn from the comfort of your home? What if you can earn $1,000 or more (per month) from freelancing by just learning few skills that will make your living.

It's not a network marketing or stock trading scheme but the skills (in demand) that can transform your life. I'll not teach you the skills here, but will let you know the opportunities available in digital marketing freelancing.

Would you be interested in reading this book in case you want to become a digital marketing freelancer like me? Yes, you read it right. I am a woman like you and have taken this opportunity to write this book from my own experience.

Trust me, you will benefit the most, and I recommend you to read it till the end of the book (before deciding to not take the freelancing route).

The reason for writing this book is to create awareness and give the right direction to as many women as possible who are unaware of this landscape.

And even if they know, they are unable to make it successful. I am not saying that you don't do a job and try freelancing. But what if I say that you can do your full-time job and work as a freelancer as well.

These days many companies are offering such flexibility to their employees. Would you not be interested in having a side gig then?

Even if you're not doing any job or have left your job due to family conditions and limitations, you can try freelancing from the comfort of your home. This is what we will be talking about in this book.

You need to learn new skills to get into freelancing because nothing comes easy. But you don't have to spend two decades like schooling to start earning. This is the best thing I can tell you about in this book.

Yes, I learned these skills within few months and started earning. Everything starts small and later makes a big impact. So, do not worry if you cannot make money initially, but with consistency, you'll make a good amount of money.

Once you learn the digital marketing skills, you also need to know how to send a proposal to relevant clients before you crack the deal. It takes time to understand each concept, but once you are through it, no one can stop you from earning money and living the life you want.

You'll become your BOSS and decide which projects and clients you want to work with. It feels like you have got wings to fly the way you want. Isn't it?

In this Book, you'll learn all about digital marketing freelancing, which I have been doing for a while. Let me tell you, my friend, I don't have previous experience in this field but can still make money from it.

YOU can also start earning if you read this book till the end and learn some skills that can help you monetize. This Book will help you get started with your digital marketing freelancing journey and make your first income sitting at the comfort of your home.

So, let's get started.

CHAPTER ONE

Financial Challenges Faced By Women At Each Phase of Their Life

Globally, women experience more disadvantages than their male counterparts due to damaging social and gender norms that limit their ability to access education, personal & professional development opportunities.

Many young women experience barriers to training and workforce development opportunities, including limited access to information, domestic burdens, financial constraints, poor workplace conditions, risks to personal safety, and expectations to prioritize marriage and childbearing over professional development.

In addition to the external barriers created by the society, women are impeded by barriers that exist within us. We hold ourselves back by lacking self-confidence, by not raising our hands, by pulling ourselves back when we should stand for ourselves.

We internalize the negative messages set by the society that it's wrong to be outspoken, aggressive, and be more powerful than men. We continue to take the responsibility of housework and childcare. We compromise on our career goals to make room for our partner and children.

My reason to write this book is to make each woman out there to be more powerful. Women can tear down the external barriers once we take back our power and work on our passion.

We can become our own boss. I had experienced this in my own life too which made me to write this book. I decided to talk to as many women I can, listen to their struggles, give them direction to become financially free and make their own identity.

I will be sharing my own experience too and the lessons I learned along the way. This book includes stories of women who are still struggling and trying to find their way to become financially free. The book also covers stories of women who have achieved success by finding the right direction for themselves.

Not only that, I am also sharing my journey and how I became a freelancer. You will also learn various digital marketing skills that are needed to make your living. I am writing this book for any woman who wants to be financially free and live her passion without any challenges/pressures from external barriers be it be family or corporate life.

This includes women at all phases of their life. She can be a - college student, homemaker, experienced professional or someone who wants to switch her career.

Let's take an overview of women's challenges at each phases of their life.

College Student

College days are the most memorable days for most students. But it can be daunting for some when they cannot enjoy it to the fullest. Not everyone comes from a wealthy background and won't enjoy a lavish lifestyle at this age.

Most parents give pocket money to their children for their expenses, which might not be enough to hang out with friends, party with them, do their shopping, or do anything they wish. Being a woman especially, we want to dress up well, look beautiful and whatnot. If these youngsters get an opportunity to earn some money as a side gig, will they not be able to live their lavish lifestyle?

The digital marketing skills that I am talking about has NO AGE BARRIIER to learn. You can work on different projects at any age and earn additional money for yourself.

Fresher

Now, when we move out of college, we need to find a job since we cannot be dependent on our parents at this age also. Getting a job to support ourselves becomes one of the significant responsibilities, and we might not get a job that's relevant to our qualification or we may get a job with a lesser pay.

When you're just getting started with your corporate life, there are many challenges that you might face. And many even leave their job since they couldn't adapt or are not satisfied with it. What if you can work from the comfort of your home and earn well with digital marketing freelancing? Would't you be happy doing it?

Many freshers try government jobs like banking, SSC, UPSC, to name a few. They are still dependent on their parents for their trainings and feel the pressure of not having a job or not earning money.

What if these people knew about digital marketing opportunitics and helped themselves with their coaching courses instead of depending on their parents? They can reduce their pressure of not earning money or doing any job that they are not satisfied doing.

Mid-Career

Women in their mid-career are most dissatisfied since they face a lot of office politics and don't get promotion. They might not like their job, boss, company or team and finally decide to switch company or career.

While thinking of switching career, you might end up trying different fields and still not satisfied doing them. That's why I wanted to save few years for you by creating awareness about digital marketing which has worked for many women who have switched their career or have started from scratch and made it successful for them.

Wouldn't you be interested in trying digital marketing rather?

Married

The women in this phase have multiple responsibilities in their life – taking care of their family, childcare, elder care, household chores, job, and you name it. In such a situation, work-life balance takes a toll for them.

In certain situations, women are not even allowed to work in order to take care of their family, and they must be dependent on their partners. At times, women herself wants to quit her full-time job as she cannot manage both her professional and personal life.

In such a case, a woman either has a career gap or becomes a home maker with no other options available. What if she knew about digital freelancing which she can do from the comfort of her home and still manage her family and kids? Wouldn't that be of interest to her?

Divorced

Life can be unpredictable at times, and you never know who gets into this stage. But if you are here, you must manage all your finances by yourself. Though you're mentally disturbed, you need to manage your finances in the long run.

If a divorced women is working, there are chances that she might be looked differently by her colleagues. Though this doesn't happen with everyone but still women might not be comfortable sharing all these challenges with anyone.

What if she can get an opportunity to learn digital marketing skills and work from the comfort of her home? Wouldn't that be a good option for her? She'll not be judged by people outside and can work with peace of mind from the comfort of her home.

Single Mom

At times, woman must take hard decisions in her life and keep moving on. Though it might be late, it might be the best decision to take.I am talking about single moms who had to face challenges in their life and leave their partners.It takes a lot of courage to be a single mom since you've to take all the financial responsibilities for yourself and your child.

The finances can take a toll because a child needs to be given a good education until the age, he/she can earn. It requires a lot of investment and courage to deal with every situation at this point.

What if digital making skills can help you earn good money? I wouldn't say that only digital freelancing can help but you can also try it as a side gig to earn some additional money. You can do your full-time job and do digital freelancing simultaneously to earn some additional income.

Relocated

Almost every woman relocates after marriage to be with her partner, and it can be either within the same country or a different country. It becomes challenging to get a relevant job for her experience, and she need to either switch career or compromise on the pay.

There are chances that you don't even get a job due to certain rules and regulations of governments in different countries.In such instances, all your accumulated experience goes in vain, and with time, you become a homemaker.

Stay at home can be more frustrating especially after working for many years. You might also regret shifting from profit center (making money) to costing center (costing money) at this point.

What if you can learn digital marketing skills and earn money by providing these services as a freelancer? It's ofcourse better than being a homemaker and also can help you get a full-time job once you've enough experience.

This shows that at every stage of our life, starting from adulthood, we need to plan our finances to support ourselves, our family, and our career. But do we know about all the opportunities in the market? I am sure we are not.

There are many other opportunities apart from jobs that women can do from the comfort of their home, which can get them work-life balance, financial freedom, and peace of mind. In this chapter, I've given you a gist from my opinion what a women might be facing. But I also reached out to many women to know their story.

In the next chapter, I'll be sharing the real stories of women about what they have been through and what could have helped them lead a better life financially. This could give you a better insight from their learnings and experiences, which you can avoid.

• 6 •

CHAPTER TWO

Real Stories of Women And What They Want

Being a woman is complex and often unfair. Society holds us to ridiculous standards; outdated gender norms and gender pay are still widespread.

I reached out to women to understand their challenges financially since each woman's journey is different. [Note :Please note that the character names have been changed to keep their privacy]

So, let's hear from them and see if you can resonate with them anywhere.

Dakshi is a married woman who wants to run
an online business and doesn't want
to be dependent on her husband
to invest in her business

Dakshi is a woman at her 30s, she's from Assam (India) and moved to Mumbai (India) after marriage.She says, Assam is a Tier-2 city and there are very less job opportunities in this place.

According to her, not every woman from Assam can move to a different place just for the sake of job. Therefore, such woman (most probably) turn out to be a home maker. They are DEPENDENT ON their PARENTS or if married they are DEPENDENT on their SPOUSE. Generally the male counterparts continue their family business and make there living in the city.

Though she had the opportunity of moving to Mumbai wih ther spouse, she still had to face challenges. She had an entrepreneurial mindset and thought of starting a Fashion Designing business. Since she had interest in fashion designing, she thought of RUNNING a BUSINESS for the same.

She got some INVESTMENT from her husband and started the business both offline and online. Since she was living in an expensive place like Mumbai, it was not sustainable for her to continue the business. And most importantly she DID NOT WANT to BORROW MONEY from her husband again and again. Gradually she decided to LEAVE the BUSINESS.

Then she thought of teaching French language since languages were in demand in Mumbai. She learned French and started teaching it online. Here also she FACED CHALLENGES in GETTING CLIENTS for her online teaching.

There are many women like Dakshi who have passion to do something, want to be an ENTREPRENEUR (as she wants to run an online business). But FINANCES, LOCATIONS and few BUSINESS SKILLS are stopping her from making money.

Key Learnings from her experience

- You need skills which resonates with your passion
- You should have investment to sustain your business
- Find the demand in your location which you can serve
- You should have business skills eg., closing deals
- Find a skill where location is not a barrier eg., remote work

**Ananya is a homemaker
who wants to build her passion
of becoming a Make-up Artist
and create her own identity**

Every woman has a different journey, so do Ananya. She's married and having a 7-year-old son. She was a working professional before her marriage. She LEFT HER JOB AFTER MARRIAGE since her husband didn't feel the need for her to work.

Yes, there are husband (or families at times) who don't want woman to work as it can be stressful. They're EXPECTED to TAKE CARE of the HOME and FAMILY. But what about Ananya? Was she happy staying at home? NO, after working for few years, sitting at home was not her cup of tea.

Though she accepted it during her early years of marriage in order to take care of her family and kid (babies are the main reason for not doing job), now she has a BORING LIFE. Her son is grown enough to take care of himself, and she has some time for herself.

"How long can someone waste time on TV or mobile phone" says Ananya while sitting at home. She has been DEPENDENT on her husband for many years but now she wants to be FINANCIALLY FREE.

She had many ideas in her mind to get started. Her first thought was to do tailoring and later realized that it'll cause back pains and other health issues to her. She also had an idea to start online clothing business but couldn't get started because she needed many contacts and she had none. Yes, when you are at home, you don't have enough contacts or networking with people. Right?

Next idea that popped her mind was to become a mehndi artist. She felt that her locality is missing on something when it comes to mehndi, and she can offer those services to people around her. She SAVED MONEY from her MONTHLY EXPENSES and started INVESTING on mehndi materials.

She purchased organic materials and produced mehndi from it. She started providing mehndi services to few people around her. For her, word of mouth helps her to earn money at this stage and wants to scale it further.

But wait, is her family supporting her for this? As usual, most families throw their tantrums that nothing will happen, you're just wasting your time and she DIDN'T HAVE any FINANCIAL SUPPORT from them too.

BUT she wanted to CREATE HER IDENTITY, want to be INDEPENDENT and more importantly want to be able to OFFER anything that her son wants at any point of time. It gives immense satisfaction when you can offer something to your children or family from your own money.

She wanted that SENSE OF SATISFACTION by being financially free. While she got many ideas in her mind before getting started, MAKE-UP was something that she realized later. She wants to do a make-up course for which she needs an INVESTMENT (again must ask husband for it).

When you are not working, then you have to compromise on your passion too. Again, going back to the boring life and boring household routine. As a woman, we have to adjust a lot both personally and professionally.

We are capable and are willing to do more, but society and family might STOP us from achieving what we want. Ananya has so many ideas but NO SUPPORT from family to build her passion. How long can she go? Will she be able to survive the competition? Will she be able to convince her family to let her do what she wants to do?

ITS NOT EASY, but requires lot of perseverance, courage, right direction, and investment to build on her passion. She believes that PASSION is more important than money. So, if you can work with passion, you can enjoy every moment and earn money as well. So, FIND YOUR PASSION.

Key Learnings from her experience

- Find your niche.
- Follow your passion.
- Create your own identity.
- Find your passion and build it to become financially free.

**Bhavana is a married woman,
who was into teaching field earlier
and now wants to build
an online business**

Bhavana was a teacher, but she had to leave her job since her husband had to travel for his business. She searched on the internet to find some online business which she can do(while being with her husband and family).

She could not find any online business which can help her earn money. She also asked many people around her if they could help her know any good online business which she can pursue but couldn't get much of help. Most of them suggested her data entry or typing jobs and ended up landing into spam jobs.

After 5 years of search, she found digital marketing in 2019 but she COULDN'T ENROL for any COURSE back then due to FINANCIAL and FAMILY issues. She tried to learn content writing & SEO from free courses offered by Udemy and built her own website which is a digital marketing blog. But she COULDN'T FIND CLIENTS to serve them with her expertise.

She then tried affiliate marketing and trying to build her authority in the field to earn some money. Her goal is to earn enough money and support her family. She wants to SUPPORT HER HUSBAND FINANCIALLY and HELP HER DAUGHTER send abroad for her higher studies.

Though she started her journey in digital marketing, she's not able to make money due to other challenges. You can also face this problem once you get started with digital marketing.

So, my advice to you is to stick to one skill that you learn and find the platforms where you can approach your prospects and crack your first deal. I will be sharing more about the different platforms in chapter 5 and how to crack deals in the chapter 7 of this Book so keep reading till the end.

Key Learnings from her experience

- Online business is the best option to earn money if you need to travel frequently.
- Don't fall into the trap of spam emails that offer you job opportunity.
- Research on YouTube to find out what online skills are available in the market.
- Find an online business which can work for you.

- Only digital marketing skills will not help you earn money.
- Don't jump to another skill if you haven't got any results in a while.
- Have patience and keep working to get your first project.

Renu is a married woman who wants
to have her own business in future

Renu once wanted to become a teacher. She prepared for teaching exams like DSSB since she wanted to have a government job. There are many people like her who wants a government job. But not everyone can make it and many even waste years preparing for exams and not making it to the end.

Due to COVID, she had to wait for the government job vacancies for many years. When she finally got an offer, she was asked to get married. Therefore,she declined her job offer as it was in a different location than where she was based in.

She got married and had some private teaching job offers in hand which she did for few months. After some time, she became pregnant and couldn't handle schoolwork since she had to handle kids in the school. She left her job and took care of her health. She became mother of a baby girl and her whole focus shifted to raising her baby.

For 3 years, she didn't even think of doing anything but now her baby is ready for school, so Renu got some TIME to do something on her own. Thoughts of running a CLOTHING BUSINESS came in her mind and LUCKILY, she had the SUPPORT of her HUSBAND.

But when I came to know about her plans, I suggested her to have an ONLINE BUSINESS rather than a PHYSICAL STORE. I understand that many people don't know about digital marketing and still think of having a physical store.

For clothing, physical store might make sense since people like to try it out to see the fitting and all but these days, even online stores offer exchange or refund if things go wrong. There are so many flexibilities, and you can save a lot of money from renting a whole physical store.

She had plans to TRAVEL to get clothes from other locations but these days there are many wholesales available online to ship the orders for you. There are drop shipping options where people can directly send the delivery to their customers.

But NOT MANY PEOPLE KNOW about it. Since she is just in the planning stage, she hasn't given it a much research so far. But digital marketing can be a great way for her to start her ONLINE STORE.

Key Learnings from her experience

- As a woman we might have to compromise on our full-time job due to different circumstances.
- As a new mother, we don't even think of doing a job to focus on our baby.
- Once our baby is grown, it is difficult to find a full-time job and we end up doing nothing.
- Even if you have support from your family or partner, investing on an outdated traditional market can be a huge investment.
- Know the advanced technologies or market like digital marketing that can help you get started with less investment.

**Ragavi is a married woman living
in Singapore. She is ambitious
to do something in her life
and wants to be financially free**

Ragavi has two and half years of experience in visual merchandiser before she relocated to Singapore. She has keen interest in the profession as it brings out the creativity part of her. She moved to Singapore in 2019 and started searching for job in visual merchandise but faced challenges as the COUNTRY PREFERS LOCALS over FOREIGNERS.

She APPLIED for JOBS for ONE AND HALF YEARS but still the CHALLENGES remain the same. Now, she is in her 40s and her kids are 11 years old and 17 years old. Her CHILDREN are GROWN UP and now she has ENOUGH TIME to think of doing something creative and wants to be FINANCIALLY FREE.

She is flexible to learn different skills and willing to work. She DOESN'T WANT to be DEPENDENT on her husband even if he is very SUPPORTIVE.

She wants to have a BACK-UP SKILL that can help her when she has PROFESSIONAL CHALLENGES in her life – be it be a different country where she has to face challenges as a FOREIGNER or NOT HAVING ENOUGH OPPORTUNITY IN HER EXPERTISE in any location.

She feels that having a back up skills will help her do something rather than doing nothing. She doesn't like to watch Netflix or gossip with ladies but to learn different things and do something productive.

She is ambitious even at the age 40 which is quite impressive, and SHE KNOWCKS EVERY DOOR where she can figure out some opportunities for herself. She NEVER WANTED TO BE A HOMEMAKER and NEVER HAPPY SPENDING HER HUSBAND'S MONEY.

She wants to be FINANCIALLY FREE and have some PURPOSE in her life. She likes WRITING and wants to MONETIZE this skill in the long run. She also wants to LEARN DIGITAL MARKETING to figure out how she can COMBINE THIS SKILL with her INTEREST in VISUAL MERCHANDISING.

With most of the COMPANIES GOING DIGITAL, this is the best way for her to start her career back. She can also search for jobs in digital marketing in any country if she can stand out in the market or do freelancing sitting in any part of the world.

If you're flexible to learn and do something like her, then digital marketing is a great opportunity for anyone out there. I wish her to find her way to financial independence through digital marketing and combine it with her passion for visual merchandising.

Key Learnings from her experience

- Build up on your back up skills.
- If you are creative like her, find out which skill in digital marketing can bring out the creativity in you (e.g., web

designing).

- Combine digital marketing skills with your passion and work towards it.
- Have a side gig (part-time job) till you find a job in your profession.
- Be flexible to learn new skills to stand out in the market.
- Side gig can help you to be more productive and build your portfolio.
- Freelancing can help you achieve financial independence in the long run.

After having conversations with several woman, I feel that digital marketing can help them solve their financial challenges.

They can earn money to have some INVESTMENT for their PASSION. They can earn SOME MONEY rather than earning NOTHING being a homemaker. There were women who wanted to do ONLINE WORK, they can do DIGITAL MARKETING FREELANCING as their CAREER.

Most of the companies need online marketing these days, you need to find out a way how you can combine your previous experience with digital marketing to get a job or start a freelance career.

Now that you know that digital marketing can be of great help to everyone, let's get deeper into the digital marketing field in the next chapter and know what skill you can learn or resonate with.

CHAPTER THREE

Uncovering Digital Marketing Freelancing Opportunities

With HALF of the WORLD'S POPULATION using INTERNET, it's no wonder that the DEMAND for SKILLED DIGITAL MARKETERS is GROWING. However, the usage of internet varies drastically across the globe. For example, according to Internet World Stats, 94% of North Americans access internet often as compared to 43% of Africans.

WORLD INTERNET USAGE AND POPULATION STATISTICS 2022 Year-Q1 Estimates						
World Regions	Population (2022 Est.)	Population % of World	Internet Users 31 Dec 2021	Penetration Rate (% Pop.)	Growth 2000-2022	Internet World %
Africa	1,394,588,547	17.6 %	601,327,461	43.1 %	13,220 %	11.5 %
Asia	4,350,826,899	54.8 %	2,790,150,527	64.1 %	2,341 %	53.1 %
Europe	841,319,704	10.6 %	743,602,636	88.4 %	608 %	14.2 %
Latin America / Carib.	663,520,324	8.4 %	533,171,730	80.4 %	2,851 %	10.1 %
North America	372,555,585	4.7 %	347,916,694	93.4 %	222 %	6.6 %
Middle East	268,302,801	3.4 %	205,019,130	76.4 %	6,141 %	3.9 %
Oceania / Australia	43,602,955	0.5 %	30,549,185	70.1 %	301 %	0.6 %
WORLD TOTAL	7,934,716,815	100.0 %	5,251,737,363	66.2 %	1,355 %	100.0 %

Internet Usage Worldwide (Estimates in 2022)

For digital marketers and marketing graduates, this rate of internet usage can give them insight where their skills are needed the most around the world. For COMPANIES around the WORLD, DIGITAL MARKETING has become the NECCESSITY, and this is an AMAZING OPPORTUNITY for DIGITAL MARKETERS to grow in this field.

Below are some top-most countries that have high demand for digital marketing skills:

- India
- Canada
- United Sates
- United Arab Emirates
- Australia
- Ireland
- Philippines
- United Kingdom

Digital Marketing is also called as online marketing, refers to the act of selling products and services through digital channels such as search engines, websites, social media, email, mobile apps etc., Essentially if any marketing campaigns involve electronic devices is considered as digital marketing.

Typically, digital marketing refers to marketing campaigns that appear on computer, phone, tablet, or other devices. Using these digital channels, companies can endorse their products, services and brands since consumers heavily rely on digital means to search for products or services.

For example, Think With Google marketing insights found that 48% of consumers start their inquiries on search engines, while 33% check brand websites 26% search in mobile applications.

This field never even existed few decades back. In 1990s, the internet revolutionized the way we communicate and how businesses started to reach their potential customers to sell products and services.

Today, any marketing campaign is incomplete without the salt of digital marketing. Internet is huge part of our lives which means digital marketers are always in demand.Marketing techniques have evolved as the consumer's consumption of information changed.

Radio advertising led to TV advertisement which then shifted to digital marketing with the rise of internet ecosystem. While TV remains the primary advertising medium for many businesses, digital marketing allows brands to reach global audience.

As the digital marketing technologies evolve, companies are adding online elements to their business to create an online presence. Most consumers these days use smartphone and research products online before buying and thus digital marketing strategies are vital to businesses.

Many companies across the globe are employing digital marketers to easily target their audiences online and many are seeing a significant Return On Investment (ROI) because of these online efforts.

While traditional marketing still has its place, digital marketing is taking over due to its affordability and analytics. Marketers can see exactly where people are coming from, what people are doing on the website, and which tactics will produce high ROI.

This data-driven approach makes it easier for marketers to work effectively and build strategies that produce high results.There are companies who are killing with their digital marketing campaigns.

Airbnb has changed the way we travel and search for accommodations. It was launched when its founders could not afford their rent, and the site now boasts 150 million users, 5.6 million listings and total valuation at 113 billion U.S. dollars in 2021.

Its digital marketing efforts lies on user-generated images and videos on Facebook, Instagram and Twitter, and popular city guides. Their Instagram campaign matches humor with exciting images of different locations around the world, making it more than just a service.

Another great example could be American Express, they have created a community of value. It leverages the value provided by industry experts on its open forum website. The forum is a collaborative website on which the brand invites guest authors from variety of sectors to share their business knowledge and wisdom. The result is content rich and popular with the search engine, all created without needing to shell money on content contributors.

Now, let's see what are the different digital marketing skills that can be monetized.

1.Content Writing
2.Search Engine Optimization (SEO)
3.Social Media Marketing
4.Email Marketing
5. Lead Generation
6. Marketing Automation
7.Website Design
8.Search Engine Marketing

Demand for Content Writing Worldwide

As we all know that the world is running on information and technology which is available at the click of a button. Every information that we find on the internet is presented in a very detailed manner to make it engaging, understanding, and valuable to the users.

This craft of making the readers experience interesting is executed by who we call as CONTENT WRITERS. Content writing is the process of planning, writing, and editing web content, typically for digital marketing purposes.

Content is the backbone of digital marketing, SEO, or any promotional idea that we want to grow online. Since content is the basis in which any business builds its reputation, content writing becomes the foundation for any kind of marketing activities.

Content writing is gaining its popularity these days owing to the diversification of areas in which one can build their career be it a freelancer or full-time job.

According to Google Trend, the demand for content writers is increasing significantly worldwide as you can see below.

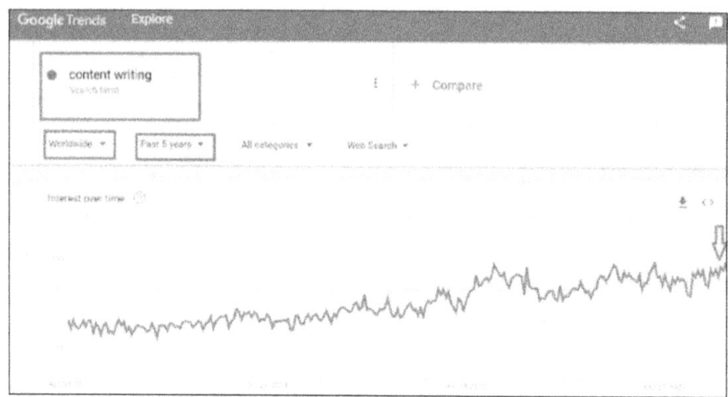

Demand for Content Writing Worldwide

There are number of options available for content writers such as blog content, website content, SEO content writer, academic content writer, video content writer, social media content writer, podcast content writer, white paper content writer and so on.

A country like India has many top content writing companies in the world. There are millions of freelance writing jobs available which helps you pay your bills while you side hustle.

No matter how far the technology advances, there is always going to be a need for content writers to express any type of information and spread it to the masses. In U.S. almost half of the labor force is now working from home. Hence rather than being limited to your city, you can begin searching for opportunities around the world.

Savvy companies are also realizing that they can hire freelancers for certain jobs such as content writing and copywriting, where they can pay them well and still have less expense than hiring a full-time employee.

And believe me content writing is not a rocket science. Anybody can learn it and become a WRITER.

Demand for Search Engine Optimization (SEO) Worldwide

Digital world is opening doors for many businesses since everything is going digital. Even medicines and prescriptions are available online these days. But do you ever think how services like best doctors, or the best restaurants got on the top results?

Like this:

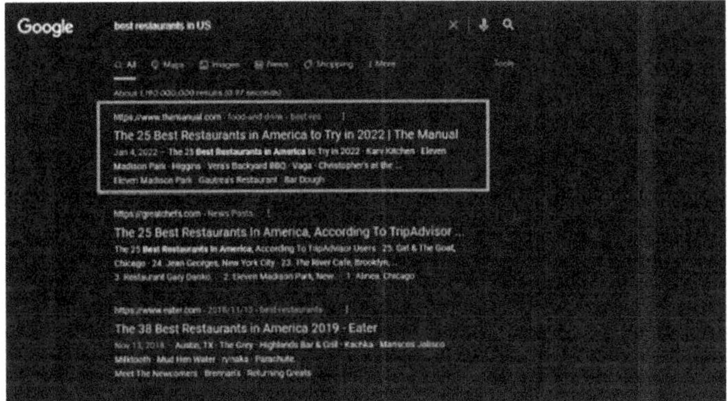

Top Search Results on Google

It's all because of SEO where the SEO professionals toil hard to bring their client's website on the top organic search results. SEO, or Search Engine Optimization is the process of improving the website to increase its visibility or position in the search engines, such as Google and Bing.

According to Google trend, the demand for SEO is increasing Worldwide.

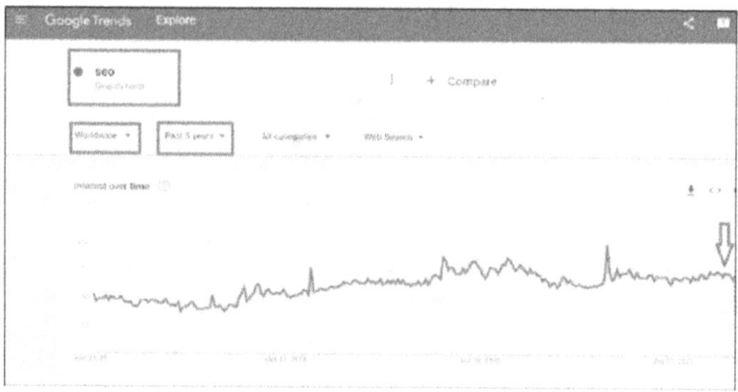

Demand for SEO Worldwide

There are about 2 billion websites in the world, and the demand for SEO is blowing up. Google dominates the game with its massive market share of search engines, resulted in $181.69 billion in revenue in 2020.

Second search engine is Bing, holding 6.7% of the search market. Other competitors are Baidu, Yahoo and Yandex. As you can see, Google is still miles ahead of other top internet search engines.

Search Engine Optimization plays a crucial role in attracting visitors and keeping them engaged while they browse on the web. On average, Google processes 3.5 billion searches per day. Globally, mobile accounted for 54.8% of all website traffic. India and China are at the forefront of the mobile revolution.

In 2021 (to date), Google accounted for over 70% of all global desktop search traffic, followed by Baidu at 13%, Bing at 12%, and Yahoo at 2%. In 2020, 55% of all worldwide online traffic came from mobile and 42% from the desktop. By 2025, nearly 73% of internet users will access the internet solely via mobile devices.

However, there is a growing demand for SEO professionals who understand how to optimize for YouTube and Amazon search. YouTube is the biggest video search engine and Amazon is the biggest e-commerce engine.

According to LinkedIn,

"As people hit the screens for entertainment and businesses in the past year, demand for digital marketing professionals (including job titles as digital Marketing Specialist, Social Media Manager, Marketing Representative, SEO Specialist) grew by nearly 33%."

SEO is an ideal career for an agile and innovative person who wants to learn something each day. The possibilities are endless when you build a career in the SEO industry since every business can benefit from it.

Big or small, online business owners are always looking for Google's first page ranking because everyone knows that almost all search happens on Google.SEO gives you a scope to work from anywhere. You will be able to get clients from all around the world.

If you search on Google, you will notice thousands of SEO experts are working as a freelancer. So, if you want to work as an individual or a freelancer, you can choose SEO as a career.

Demand for Social Media Marketing Worldwide

The number of people who use social media is expected to grow from 3.6 billion to 4.4 billion from 2020 to 2025. That's almost half of the entire planet's population scrolling through the social feeds.

Google trend also shows the increase in the demand for social media marketers worldwide.

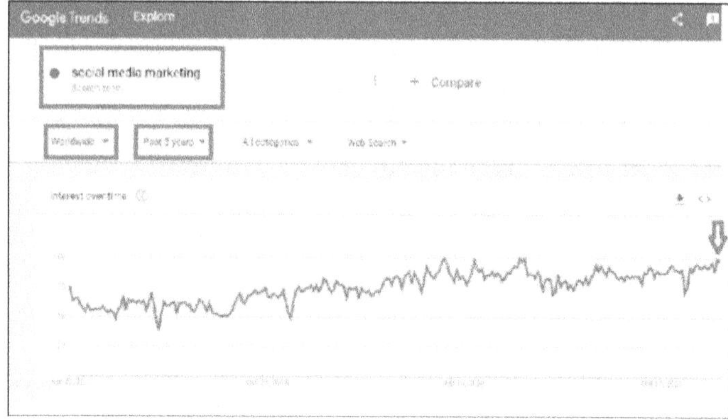

Demand for Social Media Marketing Worldwide

Social media is now an essential part of marketing services or products as customers are more comfortable buying from their mobile devices or computer rather than walking into a physical store.

There has been a vast increase in demand for marketers with social skills, with paid social media rising in demand by 116.4% according to LinkedIn data. Social media marketing is the use of social media platforms to connect with target audience to build a brand, increase sales, and drive website traffic.

This involves publishing great content on social media platforms, listening to, and engaging with followers, analyzing results, and running social media advertisements. Social media is an effective way to reach new audiences with engaging content.

Social engagement helps to build trust, authority and showcase brand personality. Social media provides huge potential for businesses because consumers log on to it daily. The most important metric for businesses is engagement and conversion rates.

Social media is more valuable to B2C (58%) companies than B2B (42%) companies. The major social media platforms are Facebook, Instagram, Twitter, LinkedIn, Pinterest, and YouTube. Social media has allowed small companies to dream of having a global reach. As of January 2022, there are 3.96 billion social media users across all social media platforms.

Let's look at each social platform one by one:

Facebook

- Despite challenges, Facebook remains the most-used platform by marketers worldwide (93%) and Instagram takes the second place (78%)
- Facebook is responsible for a quarter of all digital ad spends (25%), Google (28.9%), Amazon (10.3%) and others (35.6%) in 2020 alone.
- 1 in 3 adults consume news regularly from Facebook, signaling the popularity of latest content on the platform.

Instagram

- Instagram stories (83%) and grid posts (93%) are the most popular types of content among influencers.
- Engagement rates on Instagram are six times higher than those of Facebook.
- 44% of users shop for products on Instagram on a weekly basis.

LinkedIn

- 16.2% of LinkedIn users use the platform daily.
- LinkedIn has one of the most educated bases on social media.

Twitter

- Twitter boasts about 436 million monthly active users worldwide.

- 52% of Twitter users use the platform daily.

Pinterest

- Pinterest boasts 400+ million monthly active users.
- Shoppers on Pinterest have 85% larger shopping carts than buyers on any other social platforms.
- Pinterest users claim that platform is more influential than any other social media platform in the purchasing journey.

TikTok

- 39% of Gen Z consumer's purchasing decisions are influenced by what they see on TikTok.
- TikTok is more popular among Gen Z consumers than Instagram.

There are many small businesses or startup companies who either don't have skilled professionals to perform the basic social media jobs or simply don't have budget to hire a social media agency for their accounts.

Therefore, there is a huge demand for social media jobs from full-time to freelancing that people can apply for. It only requires you to have access to phone or a computer and an internet connection.

Demand for Email Marketing Worldwide

According to Statista data, approximately 306 billion emails were sent and received every day globally. This figure is projected to increase to over 376 billion daily emails in 2025. The number of email users are increasing day-by-day and 95% of email users check their emails every day.

It will be overwhelming to know that there are over 4 billion email users worldwide and over 7 billion email accounts. Email marketing is important because it enables businesses to build brand awareness, generate new leads, increasing product sales, building trust & loyalty with the company's customer base and increase customer retention.

Email marketing is convenient, reliable, and cost effective compared to any other marketing channel in the world. Over 90% of internet users use email and therefore email marketing is one of the best marketing strategies to promote the products and services. In addition,it is completely paperless and therefore saves huge amount on resources.

Communication is the best way for any business to grow and excel. Infact many sectors such as Banking and Finance, IT, Telecom, FMCG, etc. are focusing on email marketing to retain customers and provide personalized experience to their customers. Thus, email marketing is expected to grow at a substantial rate in the upcoming years.

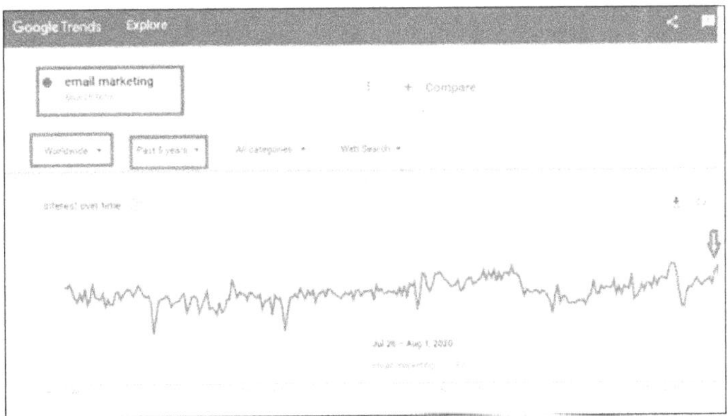

Demand for Email Marketing Worldwide

In addition, the trend towards mobile has increased the scope of email marketing, as the data shows 43% of emails were opened via mobile, desktop client share decreased to 18 percent and webmail accounted for 39 percent of opens in December 2018.

An increasing adoption of smartphones is expected to boost the email marketing industry as users don't have to open laptop or computers to access their emails. The mobile phones come with a preloaded app, or you can simply download an app from Play Store to access your emails.

Emails are now just one touch away and many people have at least two accounts these days, one for personal use and other for business purpose. The other interesting things to note is that mobile email open rate reached 81% in 2020 and nearly half of the users prefer to use smartphones to access their personal emails.

And 60% of consumers report that they purchase after receiving a promotional email from the brands. North America leads the email marketing market due to the increased penetration of technology. It has strong presence of enterprises and high degree of digitization in the region.

Asia-pacific is expected to expand at a significant growth rate during the forecast period of 2021 to 2028 due to high adoption of digital marketing solutions in the region. Developing countries focus mainly on email marketing as an important tool to improve their marketing results.

Email marketing offers several benefits to large and mid-sized business leading to the rise of adoption. And there is no sign of slowing down in the email marketing industry.

Email allows businesses to reach customers despite their geographical locations, build positive relationships with existing customer base through content personalization and increase conversions and sales.

Email marketing generates 3800% return over investment. 80% of marketers believe that email marketing is the best channel for customer retention and customer acquisition. 59% of B2B email marketers feel that email is their top marketing channel for generating revenue.

To ensure successful implementation of email marketing strategies, companies seek marketers skilled in analytics, strategy creation, copywriting, and data management. Many companies are looking to hire passionate and creative email marketers.

If your interest grows exponentially in this field as you learn more about email marketing as a career, try contacting other experts in the field who may guide you to shine in the industry.

Demand for Lead Generation Worldwide

According to SEMrush, generating quality leads is a priority goal for 79% of marketers worldwide followed by attracting more traffic to the website (75%), improving brand reputation (57%), and enhancing customer engagement and loyalty (47%) in 2020.

Lead Generation is the process of converting potential customers into qualified leads who has genuine interest in what company's offer. It is a way to funnel where potential customers move the path of buying products and services of a company.

The result is to find the qualified leads so that they can be nurtured or followed up by a salesperson. Lead generation typically involves creating content and asking for prospects contact details to receive the piece of content. There can be several forms of lead generation content that include pdf, checklist, cheat sheet, white paper, courses, free-trials, product demos etc.

Lead generation process essentially consists of three important steps:

- Attract relevant traffic to website
- Convert those website visitors into leads
- Convert leads into customers

Let's simplify the lead generation process further for your easy understanding:

Step 1 : The visitor discovers a business through one of the marketing channels such as website, blog, or social media page.

Step 2 : The visitor clicks on the call-to-action (CTA) which can be an image, button, or message that encourages visitors to take action.

Step 3 : The CTA takes the visitor to a landing page which is a web page where lead information is captured in exchange of a valuable content which can be a checklist, whitepaper and so on.

Step 4 : Finally, the visitors fill the form in exchange of a content, and you get a new lead.

The chart below shows how you can generate leads from different marketing channels.

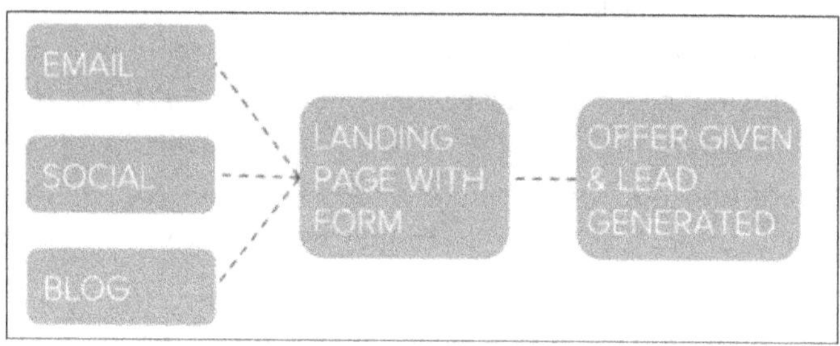

Generate Leads from Different Marketing Channels

Collecting leads allows businesses to gather information of prospective customers and nurture them through email marketing, social media or other means before reaching out to them directly to make a sale.

To grow a business, a company would need customers and marketing helps to get those customers. Lead generation is an important part of the sales cycle for any company especially for local businesses as these businesses don't have big marketing budgets or online presence.

The top industries that require lead generation are:

- Legal
- Plastic surgeons
- Insurance
- Loans and credit cards
- Home services and remodeling
- Education

- Mortgage and Real Estate
- Senior care
- Drug rehabilitation

According to HubSpot, 61% of marketers find challenging to generate traffic and leads. Lead generation is not easy and requires lot of hard work. Therefore, many small businesses, sole proprietors and independent contractors are now outsourcing their lead generation to people or company who specialize in attracting and converting potential customers.

You can build your career as a lead generation service provider to offer valuable service to other businesses. You don't have to build a product and just apply the tried & tested strategies to see the results.

Demand for Marketing Automation Worldwide

From chatbot to big data, Marketing Automation landscape is becoming more diverse every year. Customers come to businesses through multiple channels and that's why marketing automation is becoming more important than ever.

On average 51% of companies are currently using marketing automation and more than half of B2B companies (58%) plan to adopt it. According to Research and Markets Survey, the global marketing automation market size to reach USD 8.42 billion by 2027.

A study by Annuitas Group shows that companies using marketing automation to nurture their prospects see a 451% increase in qualified leads. Those nurtured leads, in turn, make purchase 47% more than their non-nurtured leads.

Marketing Automation is the use of software to automate and simplify tasks.It can save a lot of time for marketers when they follow up with leads and take the potential clients through the conversion funnel.

Tasks otherwise would take lot of time and effort that include sending drip emails, follow-up messages, adding sales calls to calendar, sending invoices, and posting on social media. Essentially whatever you need in terms of customer management can be done with marketing automation.

Here's an example:

1. Company's send an email inviting leads to attend the webinar about their product or service.

2. Leads are then directed to page to fill out a form to attend the webinar. And these leads are automatically funneled into a new email list in the automation tool.

3. Everyone in the new email list automatically start receiving nurture emails starting from a than you email to leads who attended the webinar. After few days, they receive a downloaded content on a similar topic.

4. Finally, when the leads download the content, they are automatically routed to the sales team so that they can follow up with them.

Marketing automation software often works by integrating with Customer Relationship Management (CRM) software. Marketers use these tools to personalize messages they send to leads. Companies can also schedule message and automate common responses.

For businesses with large customer database, these tools significantly increase the productivity of sales and marketing teams. Marketing automation is not limited to companies who have a huge budget or large customer base. It can make a powerful Impact on companies of all sizes, especially small businesses.

Automation helps in many ways:

- It helps to build relationships with leads and existing customers.
- Helps to follow up with potential leads to convert them into sales.
- Tracks the customer journey.
- Automates social media and reports.

- Simplifies communication with a chatbot.

According to Epsilon Research report of 2018, 80% of customers buy form brands that offer customized experiences and marketing automation helps with that experience.

Email marketing is a subset of marketing automation. The main difference is that automation is mainly for Business-to-Business (B2B) whereas email marketing is for Business-to-customers (B2C).

This is a specialized field in which many people don't have skills and it can be an added advantage if you learn it and provide as a service.

Demand for Website Design Worldwide

According to the U.S. Bureau of Labor Statistics, the demand for web designers and developers will grow at a much faster rate than the average of all occupations. According to Statista 2021, the total number of web designers and developers will reach to 205,000 by 2030.

Employment will increase by 8% from 2019 to 2029. The demand will be driven by the continuing popularity of mobile devices and ecommerce.

Web design is the process of creating a website that includes designing the layout, graphics, text, choosing the right colors and fonts. It also includes coding to make the website functional.

Web design creates a visually appealing and user-friendly website that helps businesses succeed online.There is an increase in demand for web design services from small and medium businesses (SMBs) due to the growing popularity of mobile devices, online marketing, and ecommerce.

The increasing rise of social media channels such as Facebook, Twitter, LinkedIn, Pinterest, and Instagram for marketing is also growing the demand for web design services.A well-designed website has better chances of ranking in the Search Engine Result

Pages (SERPs).

Customers worldwide need skilled web designers, and the industry shows no sign of stopping. Many companies still don't have website; therefore, web designers have many projects to manage. If you like designing, this can be a great skill to have in your profile.

Demand for Search Engine Marketing Worldwide

Ad spending in the search advertising is projected to reach USD 203 billion in 2022 and US 160 billion will solely be generated through mobile in 2026.

Search Engine Marketing (SEM) is a rapidly growing advertising strategy worldwide.It is also known as Google Ads and Pay Per Click (PPC), which is an effective way to maximize ROI. There are over three billion searches online every day across the globe and some of the searches are directly related to products and services that companies provide.

Organic rankings are not the only way to get traffic to your website, with SEM you can reach consumers at the right time (when they are already searching for the products and services).SEM allows businesses to bid on keywords on major search engines like Google, Yahoo, and Bing to drive relevant traffic to their websites.

SEM campaigns allows businesses to show their ads to people in specific location who are already searching for specific key phrases or words. Organizations are only advertising to people who are looking for something that these businesses can provide.

Advertiser bid for a limited space available on the SERPs.Clicked ads lead to targeted content that can be a product purchase page, an informational page, newsletter, app download or other actions with value for the business.

SEM campaigns can be tracked at every step from impressions to conversions and everything in between. This allows experts to determine the effective ways to run the campaign and get the best results.

SEM is the most effective forms of advertising available to businesses as they only pay when a person actually clicks on their ad. Google Ad and Facebook Ads are currently the biggest search advertiser on the market with 37.2% and 19.6% market share respectively.

In addition to Google and Facebook, there are other PPC platforms that include Amazon, Twitter etc. The SEM industry is on rise and both companies and service providers are profiting from it. There are around 1,600+ remote jobs available for Search Engine Marketers around the world and this skill is required by almost most of the companies out there.

If you are wondering how long it takes to become a digital marketer or expert in any of the specific skills mentioned above, let me tell you that you don't have to wait too long to become an expert.

It took me less than 6 months to learn one of the skills and start working on various projects. I am not trying to boast about myself but telling you the truth from my experience. And anybody can get started in such a short time.

We invest a minimum of 16 years in our schooling to get a full-time job, but digital marketing does not require that much time. And it has worked for me.Digital marketing is more about practical skills than theoretical skills and you can learn those skills to become a successful digital marketer.

Additionally, as a digital marketer, your career can take different paths – you can become freelancer, start your own agency, or work for any company.

In the next chapter, I will show you how women have succeeded in all these skills and having a successful career in the digital marketing industry.

CHAPTER FOUR

Case Studies of Successful Women Freelancers

Now that you know the huge opportunities available in Digital Marketing, let's look at some of the women entrepreneurs who have build their career in digital Marketing.These women have proven results in their own field of digital marketing.

The reason for sharing their story is to inspire you and remove all the blockages that you might have in your mind regarding freelancing in digital marketing.With the overwhelming information available on the internet, there's no doubt that it can seem to be another quick get rich scheme to many.

That's the reason for sharing the real stories of other women to make you believe that this skill can help you monetize at the comfort of your home. So, let's get to know them.

Hansika is a young woman
who kicked her full-time job
and became an Affiliate Marketer
(Her goal is to become an Online Business Coach)

Hansika is a young woman who just started her career. She passed her college 2 years back (2020) and got placed in an ecommerce company. She was not happy with the work that she was doing since it had no scope of growing within the company or getting better opportunities in the market.

Like many others, she had an impression that MBA is required to get better opportunities and big package. But doing MBA from a renowned university was more important than just doing an MBA from anywhere.This made her to prepare for CAT exams and appeared for it.

Inspite of getting 81 percentiles, she was not confident that she could get any good college since the competition was very high. And to get into a good college otherwise was costing her 14-15 lakhs which is very expensive.

After realizing that MBA is not going to happen, she joined a marketing agency where she got a good package. She could continue the job more than 4 months due to the work pressure. She used to work for 12 hours which made her to take a strong decision of not working for anyone.

The initial years of bad experience can change our opinion and the way we perceive them. These are the lessons that mold us to become the best version of ourselves. She started to learn skills through YouTube videos and took some digital marketing courses.

The best part was she had saved money from her past work experience which helped her to take her decision. Through YouTube, she came to know about affiliate marketing opportunities. She came across an expert in the affiliate marketing industry who was part of her digital marketing course as well and gave her directions to get started.

She also started content writing when she connected with many people through her affiliate marketing journey. She earned $1000 dollars in less than 6 months through affiliate marketing and now her goal is to become a business coach where she can teach other businesses on how to get them started.

Look at her transformation, being a young woman starting her career in the wrong place then decided to not work for anyone and becoming one of the successful affiliate marketers and aiming to become business coach.

This was possible for her since she had some investment which she can put on her learnings and match the market demands. If you want to be your own boss, then you need the skills that can help you achieve it.

She found that affiliate marketing is something that can help her achieve her goal of becoming a business coach. But she has a great advice to share with all of you. Though she started searching on YouTube to learn skills, she realized that you cannot rely on YouTube to grow yourself. You need a mentor to guide you through.

Let's take her example itself, she says that by watching YouTube, she was able create a website and started blogging, but she could not get any traffic, she created an Instagram handle with posts on quotes to drive traffic to her website but that didn't work.

She tried to create compilation videos on YouTube to get traffic to her website and that also failed. That's how she realized the worth of having a mentor. She achieved success when she had a mentor who can see her challenges and how to take her in the right direction.

As of now she has only invested 20% of her savings on learning and was able to achieve great profits from it. When I asked her what if her coaching business didn't work, what will she do then?

Her response was that she will do copywriting or social media which is also part of digital marketing. As I mentioned earlier, digital marketing has lot of opportunities, if one doesn't work, you can still take up other opportunities.

Another great advice that she has for all of you is build your personal brand on LinkedIn and Facebook. Based on her experience she has realized that people buy from people and if you are the leader in your field then people will buy from you.

Follow any one platform and try to build your brand by posting some valuable content which attracts and inspires others to follow and trust you. Keep learning till you figure out what you want to do.

Key Learnings from her experience

- Build your personal brand on LinkedIn, Facebook or wherever your prospect hangs out.
- Follow one platform and build your brand.
- Do not depend on YouTube alone to achieve your goal.
- Have a mentor to guide you through your challenges.
- If you don't know where to start, keep learning till you figure it out.

**Sana was a production engineer
and a skin-care blogger by passion
who turned her passion into a profession.
(She is now a professional blogger
and content writer on which
she monetizes and makes her living)**

Sana was earning well with her full-time job, but she was not interested to continue it as she felt it as a monotonous job of working with machines and decided to be her own boss.

She learned skills from YouTube and took some web designing courses before she could provide Graphic Designing (logo designing, template designing etc.) and Website Designing service as a freelancer.

It worked well for her, and she still sells them as a digital product. She wanted to scale her skin-care blog also, but she was not able to get traffic to her website, so she started watching YouTube videos and joined digital marketing courses to learn different ways to increase traffic to her website.

Once she learned digital marketing skills, she decided to become a content writer freelancer. She felt freelancing exciting and at the same time thrilling also. Earlier she was blogging only on her own website which is a different experience and writing for clients is completely a different ball game.

As a content writing freelancer, she had to send cold emails, share samples, and submit proposals before she could get a project. That was a different experience but overcame the challenges with her experience.

But once you get started as a content writer, it is a beautiful profession to be in since you also learn multiple things while writing on a particular topic. She now not only writes for national clients but also for international clients.

She says that finding the write client is more important who can pay the right price for your work. There are many communities she is part of but not all clients pay a good sum of money. So, she suggests packaging your offer as a service which many clients like to agree.

For example, offer x number of articles combined with social media copies and converting blog as a newsletter. This is just an example; you can be good in other skills which you can offer as a package.

She also follows influencers on Instagram from where she finds some clients to pitch them for her services. Additionally, she sends cold emails to decision makers of the company on LinkedIn.

Decision makers can be content managers or anyone who handles the content for the company. And you can only be part of different freelance platforms like Pepper Content which is a platform for content creators.

There are other freelance platforms like Upwork, Fiverr to explore. First thing you need to ensure is to be specific about your niche and at least stick to it for one year and then expand to another niches.

This way you become expert in one field and then scale your service later. She advices to have patience with your work since you might not get results in a month or two but keep working even if it takes 6 months.

Once you crack your first client, it becomes easy to keep moving forward. She also gives us a valuable nugget for women who have technical background and not able to continue their job for some reasons.

They can start as a technical content writer since it requires technical expertise. For example, Saas writing is in demand which not all writers can write about. Based on her experience she feels that Skills based professionals are in demand especially during COVID so keep learning skills and provide them as a freelance service.

Her long-term goal is to become a content strategist or a consultant which she will make once she has enough experience. What is your goal? Do you have some clarity where to start now? Believe me content writing is not a rocket science and you can also get started from the comfort of your home. So, pick a niche and start working on it.

Key Learnings from her experience

- Find your niche.
- Stick to your niche for at least one year before expanding to other niches.
- Content writing also helps you to learn on different topics while serving clients.
- Offer services as a package to attract more clients.
- Do not lower your worth and work with right clients who offer best price.
- Pitch your services to decision makers in the company.
- Send cold emails to your prospects where they hang out such as LinkedIn, Instagram etc.
- Explore different freelance platforms (Pepper Content, Upwork, Fiverr etc.,) where you can offer your services.

Padma was a Civil Engineer by qualification
with no work experience before she relocated abroad.
She was always interested in digital marketing and
learned the skills which helped her to get a full-time job
(She has plans to start freelancing in future)

Padma was just a graduate when she got married in 2016 and relocated to US. She comes from a civil engineering background and faced challenges getting a job in US. Being an Indian national, not getting a job in different country is very common especially when you are not into IT field.

Padma applied for 100-200 companies and was interviewed by around 50 companies but couldn't get a job there. Government in different countries does not allow companies to hire foreigners since they want to employ more locals to grow their nation.This becomes a challenge for people who are seeking job in other countries.

She wanted to do higher studies to get a job in US, but it was expensive. It costed her around 25 Lakh in INR and didn't want to ask her husband for it. For one year (2017) she did content marketing for her spouse's job portal website and later moved back to India in 2018 for her higher studies.

She did Post Graduate Diploma in Data Science which costed her 10 lakhs in India. This is a huge fee that her husband paid for her but unfortunately not everyone is privileged to get such a support. After a year, her husband also moved back to India, and she thought of trying jobs in the home country.

She was based in Bangalore and tried few jobs but unfortunately got offers from other cities. She had to refuse them as family was not ready for her to move to a different city for her job. In 2019, she moved to Singapore along with her husband and same challenges she had to face as she did in US.

She applied for some remote jobs and got an opportunity for an unpaid internship. She did it for one year and moved to Australia in 2022. Though she started digital marketing (content marketing) without knowing where it is taking her, she got an opportunity to work in a company in Australia.

She realized that her education has not helped her much even after spending lakhs of money. She likes what she is doing now (digital marketing) and has plans to do digital freelancing in future.

Even if you want to do a full-time job, you can try freelancing as a side gig. And freelancing will always be a great asset to have especially when you relocate to a different city or even country. There are many women who are facing challenge with their full-time job since their spouse must travel for their work.

In such a situation, women decide to leave their job to stay with their spouse. We as a women keep compromising on many things. But given an opportunity like freelancing can be a great way to help ourselves in many ways – be it be financial independent, build our own identity, be a support to our family financially and help ourselves to build on our passion without being dependent on our spouse or family.

Key Learnings from her experience

- Keep learning even if you don't know where you are moving towards
- Find your interest and work on it
- Don't lose hope if all doors are closed
- Work even if you aren't paid initially to build your skills
- Digital Freelancing skills doesn't cost you lakhs of money (like your Bachelor's and Master's course)
- Digital Freelancing can be a great asset if your spouse is travelling for his work

**Prachi is a strong woman
who has seen all the odds in her life
and bounced back to build herself again from scratch.
(She runs a digital marketing agency now)**

Before I share her story, I must say that she deserves a big shout out from all the women out there. I hope you will agree with me by the end of her story. I had a conversation with her twice to understand her entire journey and let me tell you that it takes a lot of courage to share a failed relationship which she did.

I am thankful to her for trusting me and sharing her story with me. I have known people around me who I have known but they were never comfortable sharing with me. I always wanted to help them, but it seemed that they are so much disturbed in their personal life that they are not able to come out of it. And that's where Prachi stands an inspiration for all such women.

I understand that everyone has their own ups and down in their life but unless you try to show courage to find the solutions for it, you will never move forward in your life. Your life is precious, and everyone is unique in their way. Be the best version of yourself no matter what challenges you need to face in your life.

Your life is in your hand, and YOU have the power to change it the way you want. So, let me share PRACHI'S INSPIRING STORY with you all. Prachi started working when she was in second year of her college back in 1999. She got a job through her uncle in a college where she worked for 6 months without salary.

For her money was not an issue as her father was a central government employee and earning well for the family. She focused on her learning and quit her job when she was in 3rd year. She did an ecommerce course after that as it was booming in those days.

She also learned programming languages like C++, Java, HTML etc., After her M. Com, she started her full-time job at Reliance as a Broadband Manager. She got hike within a year for her good performance.

She later worked in other companies like Airtel and CitiFinancial. Things were going well during the initial years of her career. Later, she got married to a rich family and left her job since she could focus on one thing at a time.

Her spouse's family also wanted someone who doesn't work. Prachi decided to be a home maker. Within a year, she got pregnant and became a mother to a baby girl. Her spouse and his family weren't happy about the baby girl though.

She got pregnant again and this time family wanted to check if it's a boy or girl. It was a girl and the family asked her to abort the baby. It's not easy for a woman to abort a child but she did it. It was not the only time that she had to abort.

Every alternate year, she became pregnant and was asked to abort since it was a girl. It was a complete torture for her and inspite of being married to a rich family, things were different for her.

Her spouse was not ready to leave her for the sake of society but it's not easy for a woman to live in such a disturbing relationship.

She went into depression and took many migraine pills to sleep. She was hospitalized later for her health condition. She finally decided to move away from her spouse and family.

After moving out, she started her career again in 2018. She started as a pre-school teacher and simultaneously writing for Momspresso (free platform where people can write on different niche).

She also did digital marketing course in 2020 to scale her skills and started taking content writing and website designing projects. She got projects from well-known people who gave her long-term projects.

She felt lucky that she's getting good projects without pitching anyone. People who've worked with her also recommend her to others who need help in their projects. Now, she's running a digital marketing agency with 3 members who are working with her on content writing and Facebook Ads.

She generated 5 lakhs in revenue in the past one year which is a good amount for someone who's just getting started. She could've stayed broken with whatever happened to her but she's a brave woman who had the courage to get out of all the odds and start again.

She has two kids to raise and took all the responsibility on her own since her spouse family was not taking care of them. She's able to take care of her kids while working 4-5 hours running her agency.

If Prachi who has seen all the challenges in her life can build herself again then WHAT IS STOPPING, YOU? I am sure you've not faced so many challenges like her, but everyone has their own problems to overcome.

Take inspiration from her. If SHE CAN DO, then YOU CAN ALSO DO. Her advice to other woman who wants to get started is start with writing on free blog platforms like Momspresso, First Cry etc., There are content writing platforms like Pepper Content where people can work as freelance writers. Follow fellow writers and read a lot to write.

You can scale to other areas once you've built one skill. She's also on a mission to help other women like her and build themselves again. She not only helped herself but wants to help other women which is quite appreciable. Being a woman, I SALUTE her for being so inspiring to all of us.

Key learnings from her experience

- No matter where you are, start again.
- Keep learning and exploring.
- Life never stops for anyone.
- Hangout with people who are better than you.
- Age is just a number. Start over again.
- Do some great work that can help spread word of mouth.

**Sarya left her job after marriage
to take care of her family
and has figured out a way to
work from the comfort of her home.
(She runs a digital marketing agency now)**

Sarya worked in the administrative line for 3 years before she got married. Her spouse's family wanted her to leave job and manage family. She was convinced as it is difficult for most of the people to manage both work and manage family.

In her initial marriage years, she was busy raising her kids and taking care of the family. She researched some online jobs at that time and found some online remote jobs as virtual assistant in social media marketing.

She was interested in working so she figured out a way for herself inspite of the limitations she had. Now after 8 years she feels that her kids are grown, and they can take care of themselves. She has enough time to do something bigger for herself.

She left her online job to upscale her skills and that's when she discovered digital marketing. Though she was already providing services in social media marketing, she had no clue what other opportunities are available in the digital marketing field.

She learned all skills from the digital marketing course and started her own agency. She built her agency in collaboration with other people who were part of the course that she had taken. She started her agency in October 2021 and provides services in social media marketing, content writing, website development to name a few.

Her advice to other women is to find the reason why you want to do digital marketing. Find out a purpose and then start working towards it. If you are just getting started, work on small projects with low budget or even for free to build your portfolio.

Once you've enough testimonials then you can start pricing your services. This strategy helped her to get full-time remote jobs which she worked for 7 years. She also advices to join Facebook groups and other forums where you can find people hiring for different projects. Example: - If you're looking for a content writing projects, find content writing related Facebook groups or other platforms where your audience hangs out.

Key Learnings from her experience

- Keep learning and exploring.
- If you're willing to do something, you can find a way.
- No obstacles can stop you from achieving what you want.
- You can work from the comfort of your home while managing family.
- Work with small budget or even for free to build portfolio.
- There are many online opportunities, you just need to research and find them.
- Learn time management to manage your personal and professional work.

CHAPTER FIVE

How To Get Started With Digital Marketing Freelancing Guide

If you are interested in pursuing a career in Digital Marketing, freelancing can be highly practical and lucrative career provided you are consistent and take the right steps. Freelancing means working independently and not as an employee of any company. Freelancers set their own hours and rules and at the same time doing productive and valuable work.

A freelance digital marketer is someone who provides digital marketing services like content writing, SEO, social media marketing, website designing to name a few and work on a project basis.

In addition to digital marketing skills, you also need to have business skills like negotiation skills, project planning and management, financial management, networking skills etc., There are chances that you might talk to ten digital marketers and get different ideas on how to get started in digital marketing.

The digital landscape is certainly vast, and you will get new ideas from each one of them. As the new innovations in digital marketing happen, digital marketers must adapt to the changes to sustain in the market.

To make it simpler for you, here are some common steps that you can follow to get you started in the digital freelancing journey:

- Find your niche
- Build your skillset
- Build your website
- Find clients
- Network with people
- Find a mentor
- Build your personal brand

Find your niche

Finding your niche might require some experimenting. You may have to get the feel of every aspect of marketing to find where you really shine. If you have time, you can do internships to see what suits you best.

You can try different internships like content writing, SEO, copywriting, social media marketing to name a few. This will allow you to get in-depth knowledge of all the possibilities available and allow you to make informed decision to get started as a freelance digital marketer.

Once you have figured out what skills you are interested in, narrow down to which industry you want to serve your expertise. E.g., Content writing for Saas companies in US, SEO for healthcare companies in Australia, Social media marketing for FMCG in Asia and so on.

Build your skillset

You may be surprised to know that you don't require a degree to break into digital marketing world.

Hands on experience is the most important thing required to succeed in the field. Building your skillsets in digital marketing is a lifelong process. Digital marketing world keeps evolving rapidly so you need to keep yourself updated with the trends and know which skills are in demand.

Learn new technologies and tools, take online certifications (initially general courses when getting started will help to find your niche). Once you find your niche, you can specialize in that profession by taking some specialized courses.

Build your website

One of the best ways to get started as a digital marketing freelancer is to build your website. This could act as a portfolio showcasing your skills like content writing, SEO, website designing to name a few.

Your website will serve as one of the greatest advertisements of your skills in the digital marketing world. You don't have to pay heavy amount on your website initially. You can get a domain and hosting which have yearly subscriptions that should be enough to get your website online.

You can use the basic themes available with WordPress which is more than enough when you get started. Later, you may wish to upgrade as per your needs.If you are someone who likes writing, you can take up blogging on your site.

It's a relevant skill to have in digital marketing and you can get started quickly without having to source any clients. You can showcase your writing style, industry knowledge through your blogs to establish yourself as a brand. Your website and stories you tell is a great way to entice prospective clients.

Find Clients

This can be the most difficult part when you get started as a digital freelancer. But according to Upwork, the freelancing industry in the United States itself accounts for over $1 trillion of income every year making it the larger part of the economy.

There are several freelancing platforms and social media platforms to get started. To make it simpler, you can look at the below options to get you started as a freelancer.

Upwork or Fiverr

These are online freelance platforms catered for freelancers. If you don't have a portfolio, you can start with small gigs that will help you build it.It's important to note that these platforms charge some percentage of commission based on different projects, so you need to be cautious of sending proposals to clients.

Shortlist clients that meet your expertise and bid for those projects.It is not necessary that every client respond to your proposal, and you will get those projects.

Also ensure that you add the platform commission fee into your bidding cost so that you don't have to pay from your earnings. For example, if you bid for a $50 project, Upwork will take a 20% commission from it.This means you will receive $40 in your pocket instead of $50. While on the other hand, if you add Upwork commission fee into your bidding and bid for $65, you will receive $52 in your pocket.

Facebook Groups

There are many Facebook Groups for freelancers. These are the communities that provide relevant information about clients searching for freelancers and people seeking freelance projects.

This helps to connect the right clients and freelancers to work together. Initially you can work with low-cost projects to gain some experience and build your portfolio. Once you have the confidence and have a strong portfolio, you can start charging high and make a living with your freelance career.

LinkedIn

LinkedIn is the largest professional network and is great for making connections, building relationships, and finding job opportunities. Post on LinkedIn about your freelance services and make sure that your bio states that you are a digital marketing freelancer.

LinkedIn helps to spread the word about how you can benefit the businesses seeking marketing help. You can also create alerts to get notifications of the type of projects that you want to work. Send cold emails or cold pitching to potential clients. It is one of most traditional methods freelancers use to find their clients and it still works today.

Don't undersell yourself or your work when reaching out to prospective clients, but make sure you aren't rigid when it comes to negotiation especially when you are starting out. You also need to know your worth and you should certainly aim for better paying projects that will boost your career and transform your small business into a thriving one.

Internshala

Personally, I feel Internshala is a great place to start and experiment different skills.It is a platform which offers internship opportunities and jobs to freshers seeking for a job. You can work as an intern or full-time for some time till you build your skills and portfolio and then seek for freelance opportunities on other platforms.

Internshala has many opportunities for different levels of experience, offers short term and long-term projects, flexibility of number of hours you work depending on different projects and you get a chance to work with CEO and Founders of the company directly.

You can experiment with short term projects like one month or two months to see if you find it interesting or not. If not, then find another project and do the experiment till you find the right fit for you. Please note that you can find both free & paid internships here. In addition, if you are seeking full-time paid job for some time, you get the opportunity to find that too.

Network with people

One of the best ways to boost your career is to network with like minded people like other digital marketing freelancers. This will enhance your professional network and add value into your business. Meet people offline or online, join freelancing groups on social media like Facebook, Instagram, and LinkedIn to name a few. You can also find potential collaborators who wants to work with you.

Attend networking events where you can meet freelancing professionals and prospective clients. This can strengthen your important business connections and allow you to access potential freelance projects.

Find a mentor

Having a mentor can be a valuable resource in the long run. A mentor is someone who has experience in the industry, and makes you aspire to be like them. Mentors can speak from their experience and provide you the best advice for you to succeed.

They help you reach your goal faster than what you can achieve by yourself through experimenting. You might get stuck at places when you are getting started and may end up leaving what you wanted to do. A mentor can be a great guide at this point and help you remove all the blockages.They provide you the right direction and take you to your end goal.

Build your personal brand

Use the power of social networks to build your brand.Create personal pages on LinkedIn, Instagram, Twitter, Facebook and start connecting with other professionals. To increase your follower base, make sure that your profile describes who you are and what you do and publish relevant digital marketing content on your pages. If you build your personal brand, you can stand out from other freelancers and get better projects.

CHAPTER SIX

My Story

I was always ambitious to do something that satisfies me. I never wanted to compromise on anything in my life - both personally and professionally. I like to give my 100% in anything I do. Like most people, I had my own ups and downs during my journey and I am sure many people can resonate with me.

I was an Electrical and Electronic Engineer by qualification but never wanted to start my career in the filed. Honestly I never understood what I learned in my engineering days (lol). I didn't knew what I wanted to do in my life (during my college days).

I started my career in the marketing industry. I applied for different jobs and got this opportunity as it just happened to me during my journey. I believe in keep doing whatever comes your way and one day you'll be able to connect the dots.

I started my marketing career in 2013 just after passing out from my college. I was never satisfied with my job to be honest. But I NEVER STOPPED exploring. I tried different verticals of marketing, tried programming course (to try software jobs), banking course (to get a banking job) but I FAILED. It didn't stop me from trying even harder.

I DIDN'T GIVE UP. I kept exploring while continuing my career the way it was taking me and came to know about digital marketing which actually attracted me. I did a course again but I FAILED. I thought of giving up but something changed in my life which drived me to try it again.

I got married and moved to Singapore. I never knew that it can turn my career upside down. Getting a job and that too in marketing is not easy when you are in a different country (unless there is a huge scope in marketing in the country and they hire foreigners).

My experience didn't help me get a job in Singapore. I applied for many jobs and got only rejection mails. It's quite disappointing to see so many rejection mails and makes you feel that you're not fit for a job. But that's not true.

Different countries have different rules and they prefer locals over foreigners. Companies have few quotas to hire foreigners and need to pay certain pay scale to hire them. Due to so many restrictions and limitations from the respective country's government, it's not feasible for companies to hire a foreigner. It has nothing to do with your skills.

The only way to find yourself a job in a different country is to stand out in the market. That's when I started upscaling my skills. I researched which skills are in more demand and how to survive in the market. That's when I circled back to Digital Marketing. It has a huge demand all over the world and not just any specific country.

I learned various skills in digital marketing and started freelancing in it. It was not easy for me but when I felt that all doors are closing, I had to create my own way. That's when I discovered Digital Marketing Freelancing. I prepared myself to be market ready within 3-4 months and started managing different projects.

I learned various digital marketing skills namely content writing, copywriting, SEO, social media marketing, website designing and marketing automation one at a time through various specialized courses. I handled different projects simultaneously while learning all these skills.

In 2020, I built my website - www.digitaljayasty.com , a digital marketing focused blog. [I also have another website - www.jayasty.com, which was earlier a blog and now a WooCommerce store]

These are sites are my digital assets and acts as my brand which showcases my writing style, website design style (I designed few pages on Elementor Pro) and other digital skills which makes it easier to display to my prospective clients.

So, do you have a question in mind that how did I get started and scaled my digital marketing freelance carrer?Don't worry! I'll be sharing everything with you here to help you get some insights from my freelancing journey.

I started with content writing internships from Internshala which helped to me build my writing skills. I don't have any content writing experience earlier and started with a simple english literacy. Honestly anyone can get started with content writing and learn while writing.

Many people have that mental blockage that they cannot write, they don't have a good english etc., but trust me I don't consider myself to be a good english speaker or eve a writer but I have written 300+ articles across industries.

When you are getting started and experimenting skills, Internshala is the best place to explore. It helped me land many internships which built my portfolio. Apart from that, I created profile on freelance platform like Upwork which helped me with content marketing and SEO projects. You can also try other freelance platforms like Fiverr, People Per Hour, Freelancer and LinkedIn is also a grat place to get freelance projects.

Networking with people on different communities also helped me get multiple projects. Connect with people on social media like Facebook Groups, Forums and other social media platforms.

All skills that I learned gave me good returns and motivates me to keep learning and grow my business. After exploring different areas of opportunities like software, banking etc., the only place that I could find faster returns was Digital Marketing.

I learned all these skills from the comfort of my home and started earning. I can guarantee that you can also get more returns than what you might invest in learning these skills. It has definitely worked for me and that;s the reason I wanted to help you too.

If you're not convinced yet, then let me share my work that will speak for me. Here are few of my internships that helped me build my skills and portfolio:

Internships

Content writing Paid Internship

Skepsi Software Private Limited
715A, 7th floor, Spencer
Plaza, Mount Road, Anna
Salai, Chennai, 600002

TO WHOMSOEVER IT MAY CONCERN

Date: 23rd Mar 2021

This is to certify that Jayasty A, has successfully completed her internship with Skepsi Software Private Limited during the period 22th February 2021 to 23rd March 2021.

During the period, she wrote blogs on Artificial Intelligence, collaborated with other team members and wrote 5 blogs per day.

During the course of internship, Jayasty A has shown great amount of responsibility, sincerity and a genuine willingness to learn and zeal to take on new assignments & challenges. In particular, her coordination skills and communication skills are par excellence and her attention to details is impressive.

We wish her all the very best for her future.

With regards,

Mahipal Rajpurohit

Project Head

Enter Caption

Date: 02nd April 2021

TO WHOM IT MAY CONCERN

This letter is to certify that Jayasty Anandan has successfully completed her internship program of five weeks with us. Her internship tenure was from 15th February 2021 to 23rd March 2021. She was working with the Content & SEO team. She was assigned the task of writing content for our website & for network websites.

During the internship, we found her to be punctual, sincere & hard working. She delivered the tasks assigned to her on time. We wish her a bright future.

Sincerely,

Manager – Human Resources
31West Global Services

SEO Paid Internship

Date: 16th June 2021

Certificate of Experience

This is to certify that Jayasty Anandan has completed her internship as a Digital Marketing Intern with Blacaz. Insurance. Her internship tenure was from 1st April 2021 to 25th May 2021. As part of her internship, she handled projects on SEO and Brand PR.

During this period, her services were found to be satisfactory in carrying out the following duties:

- Auditing existing website.
- Performing ongoing keyword research including discovery and expansion of keyword opportunities
- Research and implemented content recommendations for organic SEO success.
- Maintain reports and provide analysis to help identify trends and opportunities.
- Competitive research and benchmarking.
- Content writing and optimization.
- Optimizing pages for search engine optimization.
- Research and develop new media contacts, update database, and press lists.
- Identify media opportunities for print, online and crafted media outreach email pitches.

She worked sincerely on her projects and her performance was rigorous, organized, and very efficient in her work.

We wish her all the best for her future endeavors.

Sincerely,

Maxime BERGER

Operations Leader & Co-founder

BLACAZ. Pte Ltd

Social Media Marketing Unpaid Internship

Freelance Projects Testimonials (Upwork)

Content Writing Projects

Content for My Company Website

★★★★★ 5.00 Nov 6, 2020 - Nov 21, 2020

"AJ is absolutely great to work with, good communication, and great results. I recommend her and will defiantly use her services again."

Do You Have a Personal Blog/Website? Get Paid to Post on Your Own Blog or Website!

★★★★★ 5.00 Sep 8, 2020 - Sep 18, 2020

"AJ over-delivered on all fronts. I was very happy with the result of her work and highly recommend her!"

Content Writer for International Company

★★★★★ 5.00 Oct 26, 2020 - Oct 30, 2020

"Great job!"

Experienced Content Writer to write in the space of AI, ML and CX

★★★★★ 4.80 Apr 25, 2021 - Jun 4, 2021

"Jayasty is very hard working. She spends good time to understand the ask of client and then comes back with very relevant stuff. God energy levels and very helpful."

Content Marketing and SEO Projects

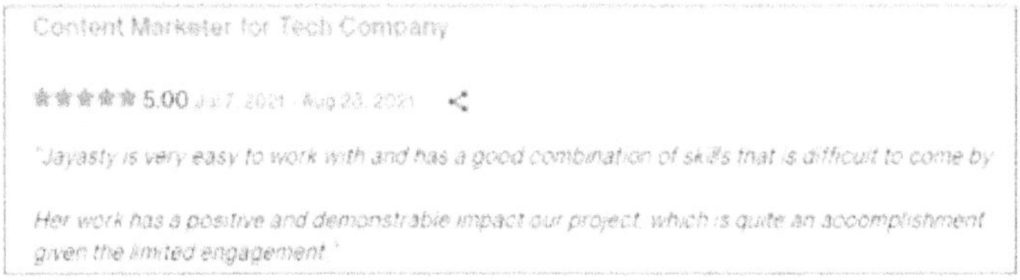

Content Marketer for Tech Company

★ ★ ★ ★ ★ 5.00 Jul 7, 2021 - Aug 23, 2021

"Jayasty is very easy to work with and has a good combination of skills that is difficult to come by.

Her work has a positive and demonstrable impact our project, which is quite an accomplishment given the limited engagement."

Singapore Based English Editor/Writer Manager

★ ★ ★ ★ ★ 5.00 Feb 19, 2021 - Mar 30, 2021

"She did an incredible job! His content and SEO search was par excellence. She communicated time to time to provide us with an excellent article. It was fun working with her. I highly recommend her."

These are few of my works and I have also worked on few offline freelance projects well. If you believe in me, I would urge you to get started with your digital freelance career. This is the best decision you will ever take, if you want to earn money and build yourself from scratch.

When you are just getting started, you can start with a small project or small budget project. I started my internship with just 5,000 INR per month and got my first freelance project for $5. I never knew if this is going to help me and how it will shape my career. But I STILL TRIED. You just need to get started no matter how small it is or even if you have to work for free in the initial stage.

With experience, I have even cracked a $500 per month freelance projects. [Remember I just mentioned that I started with $5 and now I am able to crack $500 projects too].

All this I was able to get within a span of 1 year of experience with my internships and few freelance projects. Isn't that a great achievement? If you are consistent, you can also start earning within a short span of time without any prior skills and experience.

Find a digital marketing skill that resonate with you and build your career in it. I started with content writing and then expanded to SEO, Social Media Marketing and so on. You can see my example and other women who are successful in the digital marketing industry.

Having right direction and approach is also important so find a mentor who can help you achieve your goals faster. Keep learning and explore opportunities around you. Consistency is the key to success.

Even if you are someone who doesn't want to build a career in digital marketing but build on some other passion, you can still do it for the sake of earning money rather than being dependent on your family or spouse.

You can do it as a part-time freelancer since there is no restriction on how long you work.Once you have earned enough money, you can leave it and focus completely on your passion. You can come back anytime and continue freelancing if you want, or to earn money for your passion.

Freelancing gives you the flexibility to work as you want. You can choose the type of projects you want to work. You can leave anytime if you don't like to work with any client. You have the option to either work on hourly rates or a fixed time project. If you want to take the next step towards your freelance career then we have a special bonus for you. So keep reading.

CHAPTER SEVEN

How To Close Deals With Your Clients

Many freelancers face challenges while cracking deals with clients. I have been asked this question by people frequently that inspite of having skills they get stuck when it comes to closing deals. Therefore, I have listed few questions you should ask yourself and figure out where you're getting stuck. It should act as your checklist every time you pitch a client.

Q1: Are you approaching the RIGHT clients?

Q2: Do you have a right BIO targeting the right prospective clients?

Q3: Have you created a SPECIALIZED profile?

Q4: Do you have the right PRICING for your services?

Q5: Do you have a PORTFOLIO to showcase your skills?

Q6: Do you submit YOU FOCUSED proposal to your clients?

Q7: Are you getting enough relevant INVITES?

If you are failing in any of these, you might face challenges in getting clients. To make it simpler for you, I have explained here how you can start from scratch and build your freelance profile to get more clients.

[Note: Finding the right clients, creating a specialized profile, and pricing varies from person to person which you need to identify yourself. I will not be able to cover them here but tried addressing other areas to give you some better insights].

How to create a BIO for your profile?

Clients don't care what's your qualification and how many years of experience you have.

They want to know how you can be of help to them. So, instead of talking about yourself, you need to talk about client first and then give your introduction about what you do and how you've helped your clients.

To talk about the client, you need to dig out the problems that they are facing and try to provide them a solution through your services.

Let's suppose your client is looking for a copywriter.

Your BIO could be,

Step 1: Talking about the client and targeting them clearly

Do you need a xyz (niche) copywriter? Are you a life coach who needs help in targeting the right audience and create words that move them to buy?

Step 2: Your introduction and use keywords for which you want to rank for

Hi there,

I am XYZ copywriter, and I help clients to right the exact words for the right people. I do that my using ABC techniques that helps transform minds, hearts, and souls. I work with creative startups and brands (name them if you want).

Step 3: In bullet points, mention how you helped your clients so far – it should add credibility and build your authority by mentioning the results that you achieved for them

I help clients to:

- *Craft copy that converts cold traffic to hot sales*
- *Sell $10,000 worth products in 24 hours*
- *Form the words to create lasting brand impression*

Step 4: Talk about the process you follow for your projects

When you work with me, you get faster response, clear communication and under 48 hours of turnaround time on most projects.

Step 5: Call to action (CTA)

If any of these sounds what you need, contact me.

Step 6: Signature

Kind regards,

Your name

Step 7: PS – to keep them attracted to you

PS: Regardless of who you choose, keep my profile handy in case you need me later.

Step 8: FAQs – In case you have less words in your proposal then you can add it as you should have 300-350 words for SEO purpose to rank your profile on freelance platforms and Google, otherwise its optional

Q: Do you offer email copywriting services?

A: Yes, I have worked with Active Campaign and have created outbound email sequences.

Q: Do you write sales page?

A: Yes, I've written short and long form sales pages some of which generated $10,000 in just 48 hours for my clients.

Step 9: Another CTA

If any of that is what you need, contact me.

Kind regards,

Your name

How to build a PORTFOLIO?

If you've worked with some clients, you can add the SCREENSHOT of your work say a website screenshot (showing your copywriting work).

If you want to design images for your portfolio, you can use Pexels.com which has free images and drop them into Canva to add text to it (you can use Canva's free account).

Along with the screenshot, you can add a GOOGLE DOC LINK or PDF LINK (by downloading your Google Doc as PDF) in the portfolio section.

This is because, there might be chances when the client's website might be down, and others may not be able to see it at times.

By adding these links prospective clients can see your work style, understand what you do and how you do it.

You can work for FREE when you get started and show that as your work in your portfolio. It's not necessary that you can only add work when you are paid by your clients.

You can also try to show your work on a website that you own. Your WEBSITE is the BIGGEST ASSET to show your prospective clients about your work.

Add description with relevant KEYWORDS to the work that you add in your portfolio. Have a PORTFOLIO of MINIMUM TWO PAGES when you're starting out.

How to write YOU FOCUSED proposal?

First, go through the client's JOB DESCRIPTION what they're looking for. Once you've gone through it, make your proposal YOU centric where you talk about them.

Example,

Hi there, [Greeting]

You [you centric] need a copywriter for your XYZ business preferably someone who can help you stand out in the competitive market. I write copies for ABC companies, creative brands and even startups.

Can you tell me more about your business?

[You can ask questions if you want else its optional]

- What is the biggest difference that you'd say about your brand from others?

- How is your brand's personality different from others?

[By asking questions, you show that you're competent and confident of what you do]

When you work with me, you get simple fixed rate, research included it's $100 per page up to 500 words with 2 rounds of revision (just add your rates as per your service so that clients can do their math as per their requirement). The writing will be clean, creative, and delivered on deadline.

If any of that is what you need, message me. [Call to action]

Kind Regards, [Signature]

Your name

PS: Regardless of who you choose, keep my info in case you need me later. [Your PS Statement]

How to get more INVITES from clients?

Tip #1 – Public profile

Make your freelance profile public rather than private

Tip #2 – Adjust your rates $20/hr. up and down.

Example: - Let's assume your current rate is $30/hr. Try to change it to $50/hr. ($20 up) for a week and then change it to $10/hr. ($20 down) for a week.

Check what works better for you. Changing the rates by $20 moves your profile to different price tiers based on freelance platform's algorithm.

Tip #3 – Funding milestones

If you receive a milestone from a client, it triggers other prospective clients to send you invite. Its all-freelance platform's algorithm that boosts your profile up during these conditions.

Tip #4 – Released milestones

When your milestone gets released, freelance platform's algorithm boosts your profile to prospective clients which enables them to see your profile and send invite.

Tip #5 – Top search results

Try to optimize your profile to appear on the top of search results for your niche

Tip #6 – Accept all the invites you receive

Accept invites even if you receive some irrelevant invites and send a message to that client saying it's not relevant to your skills. By doing this, you'll receive connects from your freelance platform (if they do) and boost your profile to other clients to send you invite.

Tip #7 – Apply the same freelance concepts on job platforms

Many companies post remote job opportunities on job portals like indeed, monster or other employment search engines available in your country. Freelancers do not usually look at these platforms which has a huge scope for them to get clients. You'll be paid a monthly salary like an employee but it's a freelance job for you. This helps you get annual predictable income by working few hours or as they need you to work. You can also work on other freelance projects outside these hours.

Tip #8 – Use words wisely

Never use words like Cost, Hate, Others, Risk, Impossible (in your proposal) as client's focus moves on these negative words and can decline your proposal. You need to reframe or twist the words to make it look positive to your clients.

How to get HIRED fast?

Your proposal should be YOU focused which talks about your clients, what they need, what problems they face and how your services can provide solutions to them.

FIND YOUR USP (UNIQUE SELLING POINT)

Step 1 – Find your niche

If you want to get hired fast, you need to niche down to your expertise which is basically your USP. For example, copywriting is the industry and niche will be direct response copywriter. If you go down into the sub-niche, then it can be direct response copywriter for insurance company. It makes you very specific and there might not be many clients in your expertise but those who are there will want to work with you. Because you've that unique skill that no one else has.

Step 2 – Find your specialization

What software you use for your expertise. For example, if you're an email marketer who can provide email marketing services using Active Campaign. This will be more valuable to your clients than just showcasing yourself as an email marketer.

Step 3 - Credibility

If you've any degree, previous experience, or certification in what you offer, that'll help you to stand out in the market.

Step 4 – Offer a Bonus

It can be some additional services that you can offer along with your core service.

Step 5 – Offer a Packaged Pricing

Not many freelancers offer this type of offer, but it can make you stand out in the market. Clients have the option to choose from your package.

Step 6 – Position yourself as a Brand

If you've a website, have a proper logo, colors, words, style etc. that shows you as a unique personality.

Step 7 – Have faster turnaround

Clients need to get their work done faster and if you can offer that in your service, it can help you get more projects. Example, you need not be a good copywriter but a fast copywriter.

YOU Focus + Your USP = Good PROPOSAL

What are the KEY TRAITS that clients look for in a good freelancer?

Trait #1 – Your photo

It should be clean, clear, and professional head shot photo.

Trait #2 – Title should match closely with the job post

Tip: - Change your title temporarily while sending your proposal.

Once you get the response, you can change the title as you want.

Trait #3 – Position yourself as a SPECIALIST in your BIO

Trait #4 – Good Proposal

Create a YOU FOCUSED proposal where you talk about the client and help them solve their problems.